The Night Audrey's
Vibrator Spoke

The Night Audrey's Vibrator Spoke

A Stonewall Riots Collection

by ANDREA NATALIE

CLEIS PRESS

Special thanks to my partner, Mary McClain, for her assistance, and for her Laugh-o-meter and for letting me steal two of her best lines. Also, thanks to my best friend, Pat Hughes, for her support and assistance.

Published by Cleis Press Inc., P.O. Box 8933, Pittsburgh, Pennsylvania 15221, and P.O. Box 14684, San Francisco, California 94114.

Printed in the United States of America.
Cover design: Pete Ivey
Cover art: Andrea Natalie
Cleis logo art: Juana Alicia

First Edition.
10 9 8 7 6 5 4 3 2 1
Printed on acid-free paper

Library of Congress Cataloging-in-Publication Data

Andrea, Natalie
     The night Audrey's vibrator spoke : a Stonewall riots collection /
by Andrea Natalie. — 1st ed.
        p.   cm.
     "November 1992."
     ISBN: 0-939416-64-6 : $8.95
     1. Lesbians—Caricatures and cartoons.   2. American wit and humor,
Pictorial.   I. Title.
NC1429.A632A4   1992
741.5'973—dc20   92-24313
                                                  CIP

Also by Andrea Natalie

Stonewall Riots

Andrea Natalie was born in 1958, grew up in Arizona, and attended Cornell University. She then moved to Los Angeles, where she worked as a waitress, cab driver and janitor. In 1980 she moved to New York City and came out. Her first collection of syndicated cartoons, *Stonewall Riots* (Venus Press), was a 1990 Lambda Awards finalist. Her cartoons currently appear in many gay and lesbian newspapers, including *The Advocate*, *Gay Comix*, *Girl Jock*, *Bad Attitude*, *Lambda Book Report*, *Off Our Backs*, *QW*, *Bay Guardian*, and *Real Girl*. She lives in New Jersey.

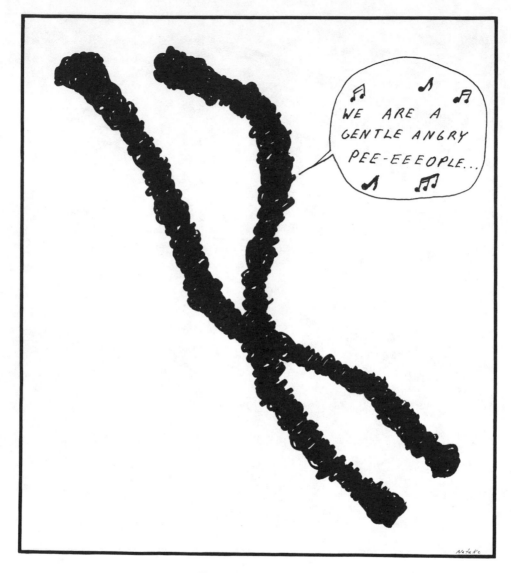

The lesbian gene

I'M GETTING MORE CENTERED BEHIND MY ENERGY. I'M STARTING TO OWN MY GRIEVING CYCLE.
I'M STRONGER. I CAN CRY.

Lesbians begin to resemble
their answering machines.

In a dark mood Radclyffe rewrote
much of her book.

After three months Toni's relationship with Joy
is still celibate.

The night Audrey's vibrator spoke.

Martha eventually confessed she'd been
letting lesbians in the house.

Lesbian logic

Linda's dental dam adhered to her face.

Kinky cats

Training bra

Dyke nightmare

Het nightmare

Biseasonal

Cereal monogamy

Lesbians in hell

"You're not the only ones, 'Rella. Our hot tub
has dykes, too. In fact, every tub in the
neighborhood's got 'em."

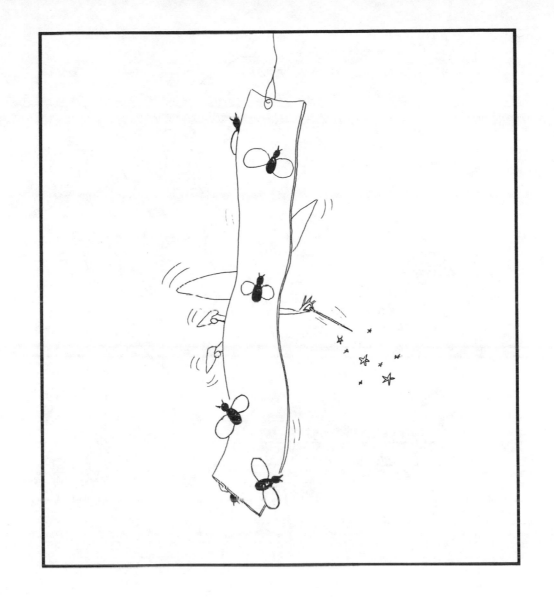

"Crystal and Amy, please read your note
aloud and tell us what your secret word,
'tribadism,' means."

How Jane and Ruth came out to the world.

Before the league banned hairspray.

The effect of male urine on Manhattan.

P.C. Patty and Big Daddy

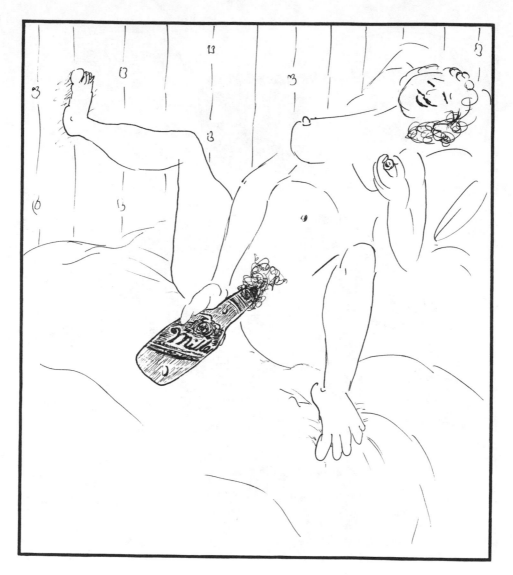

Totally P.I.

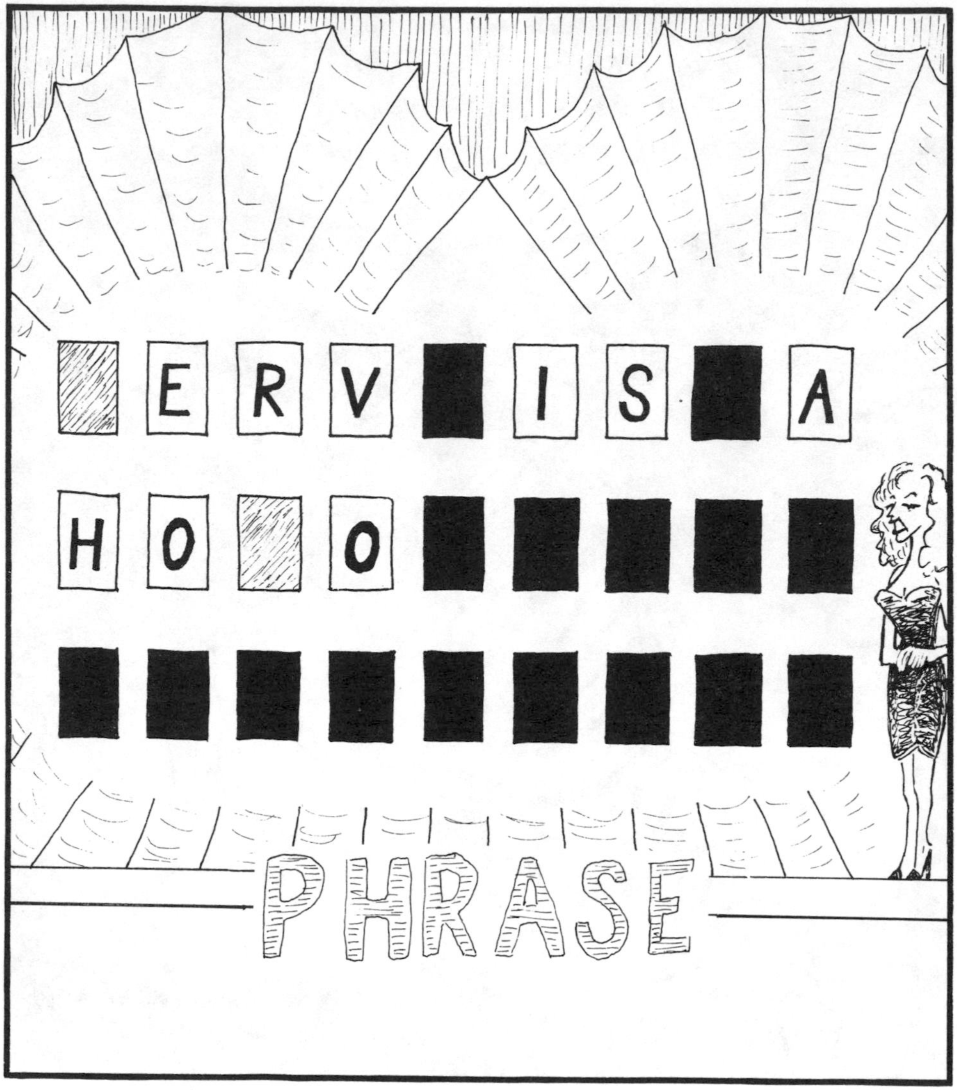
ERV IS A
HO O
PHRASE

King Fahd and his wives approach a minefield.

The "Environmental President"

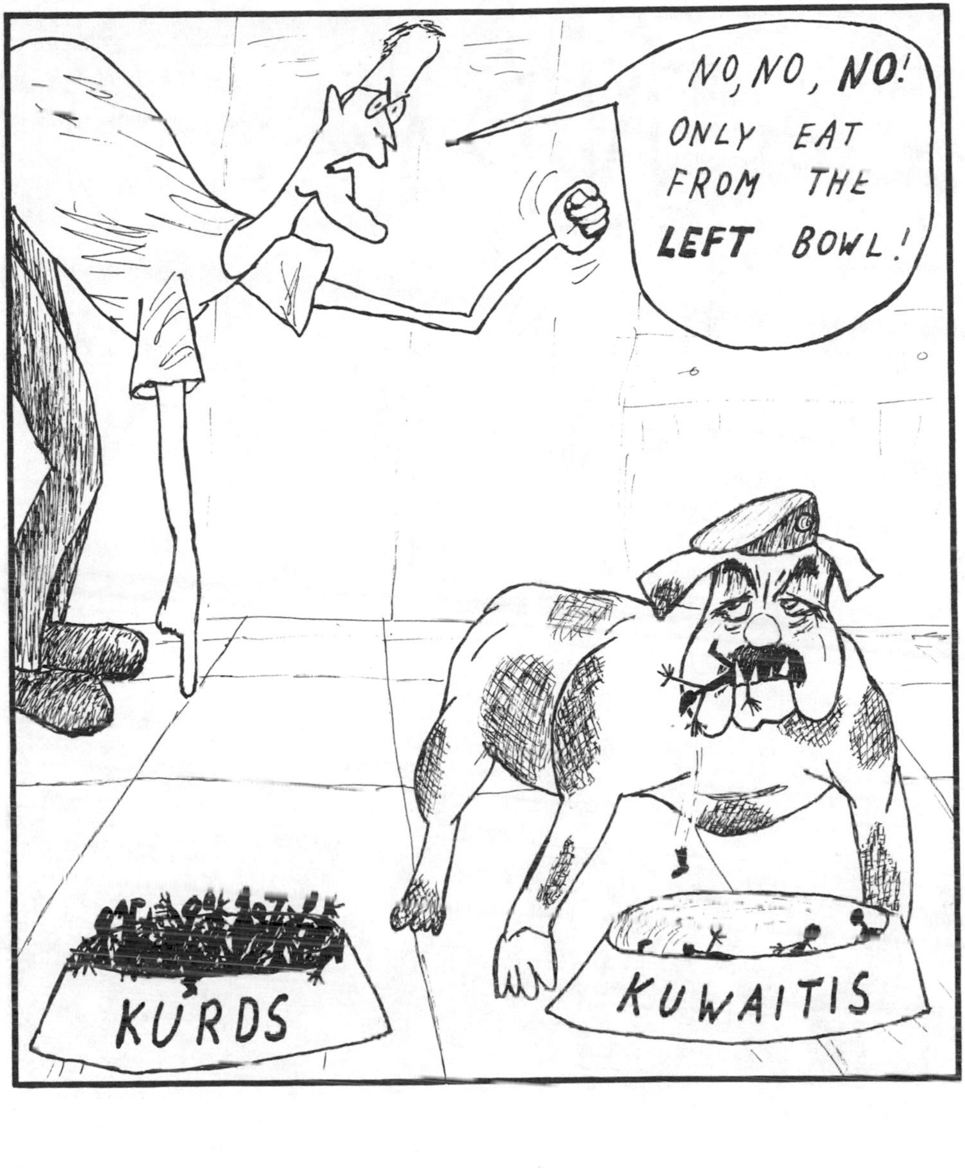
NO, NO, **NO**! ONLY EAT FROM THE **LEFT** BOWL!
KURDS
KUWAITIS

After "Thelma and Louise"

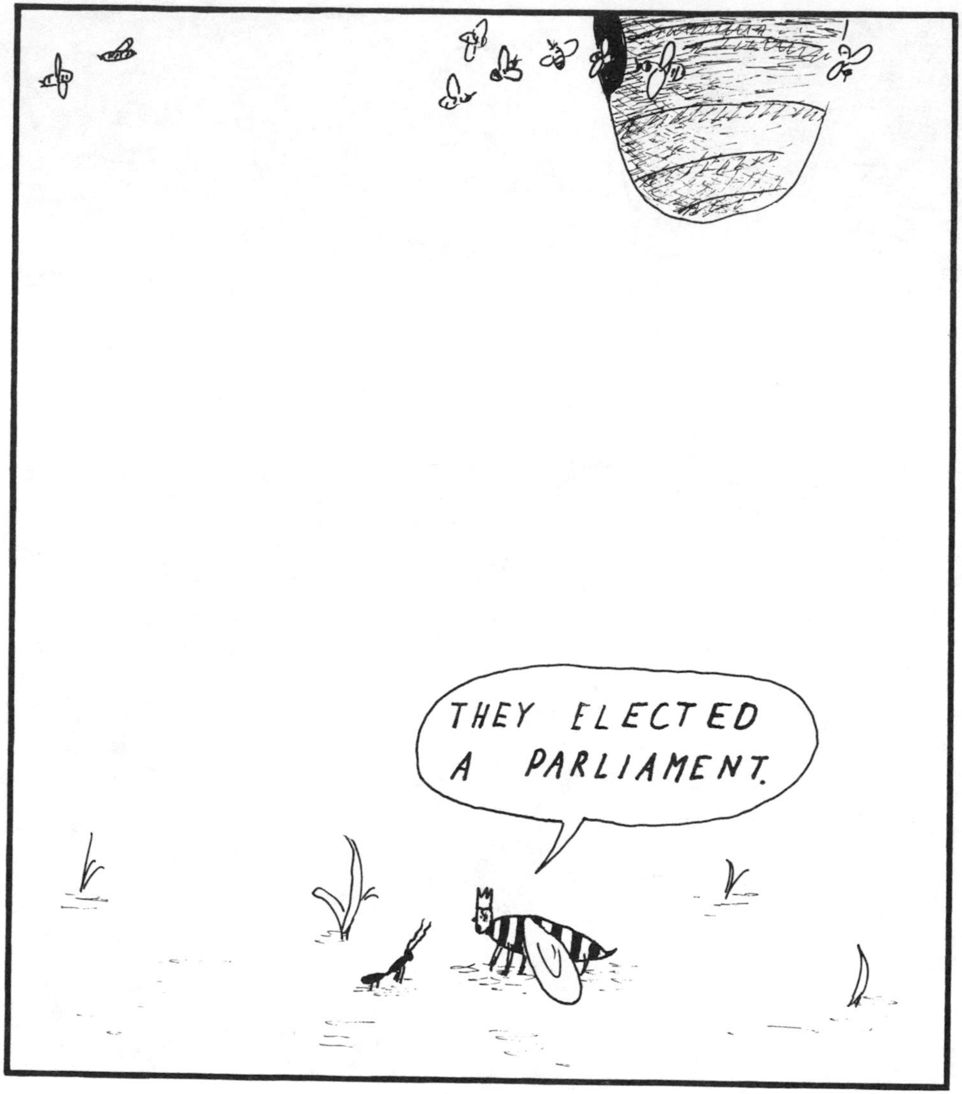
THEY ELECTED A PARLIAMENT.

HONEY, LOOK AT THIS FLYER! CAT FOOD COMES FROM B-GRADE LIVESTOCK THAT'S BRAZILIAN GROWN ON LAND THAT IS CLEARED BY BURNING DOWN RAINFOREST!
OH MY GODDESS!
ANIMAL-AMERICAN

WHEN I SAID I'D DO HALF THE COOKING I DIDN'T REALLY UNDERSTAND WHAT I WAS AGREEING TO.
CURSE YOU, MARTINA.

APPROVAL RATING
1991
DESERT STORM
1992
WE CAN'T CUT BACK ON DEFENSE! I MIGHT PROVOKE A WAR AT ANY MOMENT!

Books from Cleis Press

LESBIAN STUDIES

Boomer: Railroad Memoirs by Linda Niemann.
ISBN: 0-939416-55-7 12.95 paper.

Different Daughters: A Book by Mothers of Lesbians edited by Louise Rafkin.
ISBN: 0-939416-12-3 21.95 cloth;
ISBN: 0-939416-13-1 9.95 paper.

Different Mothers: Sons & Daughters of Lesbians Talk About Their Lives
edited by Louise Rafkin.
ISBN: 0-939416-40-9 24.95 cloth;
ISBN: 0-939416-41-7 9.95 paper.

A Lesbian Love Advisor by Celeste West.
ISBN: 0-939416-27-1 24.95 cloth;
ISBN: 0-939416-26-3 9.95 paper.

Long Way Home: The Odyssey of a Lesbian Mother and Her Children by Jeanne Jullion.
ISBN: 0-939416-05-0 8.95 paper.

More Serious Pleasure: Lesbian Erotic Stories and Poetry
edited by the Sheba Collective.
ISBN: 0-939416-48-4 24.95 cloth;
ISBN: 0-939416-47-6 9.95 paper.

The Night Audrey's Vibrator Spoke: A Stonewall Riots Collection by Andrea Natalie.
ISBN: 0-939416-64-6 8.95 paper.

Queer and Pleasant Danger: Writing Out My Life by Louise Rafkin.
ISBN: 0-939416-60-3 24.95 cloth;
ISBN: 0-939416-61-1 9.95 paper.

Serious Pleasure: Lesbian Erotic Stories and Poetry edited by the Sheba Collective.
ISBN: 0-939416-46-8 24.95 cloth;
ISBN: 0-939416-45-X 9.95 paper.

SEXUAL POLITICS

Good Sex: Real Stories from Real People by Julia Hutton.
ISBN: 0-939416-56-5 24.95 cloth;
ISBN: 0-939416-57-3 12.95 paper.

Sex Work: Writings by Women in the Sex Industry edited by Frédérique Delacoste and Priscilla Alexander.
ISBN: 0-939416 10-7 24.95 cloth;
ISBN: 0-939416-11-5 16.95 paper.

Susie Bright's Sexual Reality: A Virtual Sex World Reader by Susie Bright.
ISBN: 0-939416-58-1 24.95 cloth;
ISBN: 0-939416-59-X 9.95 paper.

Susie Sexpert's Lesbian Sex World by Susie Bright.
ISBN: 0-939416-34-4 24.95 cloth;
ISBN: 0-939416-35-2 9.95 paper.

POLITICS OF HEALTH

The Absence of the Dead Is Their Way of Appearing by Mary Winfrey Trautmann.
ISBN: 0-939416-04-2 8.95 paper.

AIDS: The Women edited by Ines Rieder and Patricia Ruppelt.
ISBN: 0-939416-20-4 24.95 cloth;
ISBN: 0-939416-21-2 9.95 paper

Don't: A Woman's Word by Elly Danica.
ISBN: 0-939416-22-0 21.95 cloth;
ISBN: 0-939416-23-9 8.95 paper

1 in 3: Women with Cancer Confront an Epidemic edited by Judith Brady.
ISBN: 0-939416-50-6 24.95 cloth;
ISBN: 0-939416-49-2 10.95 paper.

Voices in the Night: Women Speaking About Incest edited by Toni A.H. McNaron and Yarrow Morgan.
ISBN: 0-939416-02-6 9.95 paper.

With the Power of Each Breath: A Disabled Women's Anthology edited by Susan Browne, Debra Connors and Nanci Stern.
ISBN: 0-939416-09-3 24.95 cloth;
ISBN: 0-939416-06-9 10.95 paper.

Woman-Centered Pregnancy and Birth by the Federation of Feminist Women's Health Centers.
ISBN: 0-939416-03-4 11.95 paper.

FICTION

Another Love by Erzsébet Galgóczi.
ISBN: 0-939416-52-2 24.95 cloth;
ISBN: 0-939416-51-4 8.95 paper.

Cosmopolis: Urban Stories by Women edited by Ines Rieder.
ISBN: 0-939416-36-0 24.95 cloth;
ISBN: 0-939416-37-9 9.95 paper.

Night Train To Mother by Ronit Lentin.
ISBN: 0-939416-32-8 24.95 cloth;
ISBN: 0-939416-33-6 9.95 paper.

The One You Call Sister: New Women's Fiction edited by Paula Martinac.
ISBN: 0-939416-30-1 24.95 cloth;
ISBN: 0-9394160-31-X 9.95 paper.

Unholy Alliances: New Women's Fiction edited by Louise Rafkin.
ISBN: 0-939416-14-X 21.95 cloth;
ISBN: 0-939416-15-8 9.95 paper.

The Wall by Marlen Haushofer.
ISBN: 0-939416-53-0 24.95 cloth;
ISBN: 0-939416-54-9 paper.

LATIN AMERICA

Beyond the Border: A New Age in Latin American Women's Fiction edited by Nora Erro-Peralta and Caridad Silva-Núñez.
ISBN: 0-939416-42-5 24.95 cloth;
ISBN: 0-939416-43-3 12.95 paper.

The Little School: Tales of Disappearance and Survival in Argentina by Alicia Partnoy.

ISBN: 0-939416-08-5 21.95 cloth;
ISBN: 0-939416-07-7 9.95 paper.

Revenge of the Apple by Alicia Partnoy.

ISBN: 0-939416-62-X 24.95 cloth;
ISBN: 0-939416-63-8 8.95 paper.

You Can't Drown the Fire: Latin American Women Writing in Exile
edited by Alicia Partnoy.

ISBN: 0-939416-16-6 24.95 cloth;
ISBN: 0-939416-17-4 9.95 paper.

AUTOBIOGRAPHY, BIOGRAPHY, LETTERS

Peggy Deery: An Irish Family at War
by Nell McCafferty.

ISBN: 0-939416-29-8 24.95 cloth;
ISBN: 0-939416-28-X 9.95 paper.

The Shape of Red: Insider/Outsider Reflections by Ruth Hubbard
and Margaret Randall.

ISBN: 0-939416-18-2 24.95 cloth;
ISBN: 0-939416-19-0 9.95 paper.

Women & Honor: Some Notes on Lying
by Adrienne Rich.

ISBN: 0-939416-44-1 3.95 paper.

ANIMAL RIGHTS

And a Deer's Ear, Eagle's Song and Bear's Grace: Relationships Between Animals and Women edited by Theresa Corrigan
and Stephanie T. Hoppe.

ISBN: 0-939416-38-7 24.95 cloth;
ISBN: 0-939416-39-5 9.95 paper.

With a Fly's Eye, Whale's Wit and Woman's Heart: Relationships Between Animals and Women edited by Theresa Corrigan
and Stephanie T. Hoppe.

ISBN: 0-939416-24-7 24.95 cloth;
ISBN: 0-939416-25-5 9.95 paper.

Since 1980, Cleis Press has published progressive books by women. We welcome your order and will ship your books as quickly as possible. Individual orders must be prepaid (U.S. dollars only). Please add 15% shipping. Pennsylvania residents add 6% sales tax. Mail orders: Cleis Press, P.O. Box 8933, Pittsburgh PA 15221. MasterCard and Visa orders: $25 minimum— include account number, expiration date, and signature. FAX your credit card order: (412) 937-1567. Or, phone us Monday—Friday, 9 am—5 pm EST: (412) 937-1555.